AMERICA'S SONGS

I0809799

BATTLE HYMN — of the — REPUBLIC

Cavendish Square
New York

KRISTEN SUSIENKA

Published in 2020 by Cavendish Square Publishing, LLC
243 5th Avenue, Suite 136, New York, NY 10016

First Edition

Library of Congress Cataloging-in-Publication Data

Names: Susienka, Kristen, author.
Title: Battle hymn of the republic / Kristen Susienka.
Description: First edition. | New York : Cavendish Square, 2020. |
Series: America's songs | Includes bibliographical references and index.
Identifiers: LCCN 2018060557 (print) | LCCN 2018060634 (ebook) | ISBN 9781502648761 (ebook) |
ISBN 9781502648754 (library bound) | ISBN 9781502648730 (pbk.) | ISBN 9781502648747 (6 pack)
Subjects: LCSH: Howe, Julia Ward, 1819-1910. Battle hymn of the Republic. | Battle hymn of the republic (Song) | Political ballads and songs--United States--History and criticism--Juvenile literature.
Classification: LCC ML3561.B25 (ebook) | LCC ML3561.B25 S87 2020 (print) | DDC 782.42/15990973--dc23
LC record available at https://lccn.loc.gov/2018060557

Editorial Director: David McNamara
Editor: Lauren Miller
Copy Editor: Nathan Heidelberger
Associate Art Director: Alan Sliwinski
Designer: Joe Parenteau
Production Coordinator: Karol Szymczuk
Photo Research: J8 Media

The photographs in this book are used by permission and through the courtesy of:
Cover Jose Gil/Shutterstock.com; p. 4 Andriy Blokhin/Alamy Stock Photo; p. 6 transcribed by Dr. Nathan Heidelberger; p. 8 Buyenlarge/Getty Images; p. 9 American Photo Archive/Alamy Stock Photo; p. 10 Richard Thornton/Shutterstock.com; p. 12, 16 North Wind Picture Archives; p. 15 Collection PJ/Alamy Stock Photo; p. 17 Sheridan Libraries/Levy/Gado/Getty Images; p. 19 American Antiquarian Society, Worcester, Massachusetts/Bridgeman Images; p. 22 Diana Walker/Time Life Pictures/Getty Images; p. 24 Eugene Gordon/The New York Historical Society/Getty Images; p. 25 Adolphe Pierre Louis/Albuquerque Journal/ZUMA Press/Alamy Stock Photo; p. 26 (top, bottom) Philip Scalia/Alamy Stock Photo, Dia Dipasupil/Getty Images; p. 27 Paul Moseley/Fort Worth Star Telegram/TNS/Getty Images.

Printed in the United States of America

CONTENTS

Chapter 1

A Bold Song 5

Sheet Music 6

Chapter 2

The History of "The Battle Hymn of the Republic" 13

Timeline 21

Chapter 3

The Song Keeps Marching On 23

Glossary 28

Find Out More 29

Index 31

About the Author 32

When people hear the words to "Battle Hymn," they might think of truth and justice. Those qualities are often associated with the statue of this woman, Lady Liberty.

CHAPTER 1

A Bold Song

Many people have written songs about the United States. Some songs talk about how beautiful the country is. Other songs talk about how fun it is to live there. Many songs have also been written to celebrate the United States. Other times, songs help people living in the United States get through tough moments in history. One famous example is "Battle Hymn of the Republic."

Battle Hymn of the Republic

Lyrics by Julia Ward Howe

Music by William Steffe

I have seen Him in the watch-fires of a hundred circling camps,
They have builded Him an altar in the evening dews and damps;
I can read His righteous sentence by the dim and flaring lamps:
His day is marching on.

I have read a fiery gospel writ in burnished rows of steel:
"As ye deal with my contemners, so with you my grace shall deal;
Let the Hero, born of woman, crush the serpent with his heel,
Since God is marching on."

He has sounded forth the trumpet that shall never call retreat;
He is sifting out the hearts of men before His judgment-seat:
Oh, be swift, my soul, to answer Him! be jubilant, my feet!
Our God is marching on.

In the beauty of the lilies Christ was born across the sea,
With a glory in his bosom that transfigures you and me:
As he died to make men holy, let us die to make men free,
While God is marching on.

A War Song

"Battle Hymn of the Republic" is an old song. Its words were written in 1861 by Julia Ward Howe. They talk about God and winning a war. She wrote the words to help soldiers fighting a war. The war was called

The Battle of Wilson's Creek took place in 1861, the same year "Battle Hymn of the Republic" was written. This illustration shows soldiers fighting the battle. It was part of the Civil War.

FACT

The Civil War was one of the first wars where photographs of wounded and dead soldiers were taken.

This image was taken by a Civil War photographer in 1864. It shows soldiers in General William T. Sherman's unit relaxing next to a war cannon.

the Civil War. During that time, many men, women, and children lived as slaves in the United States. The soldiers were fighting to free the slaves. Howe wanted to help the soldiers when fighting was hard.

Many people heard the song's words and liked them. People in the United States have sung the song for over one hundred years.

A high school marching band plays music during a parade in California in 2013.

FACT

"Battle Hymn" is a marching song. It's easy to move to the beat of the song. Lots of people play the song and march to it at parades.

A Song for All

Today, the song is important for the United States. It is a **patriotic** song. It has lots of meanings. Some people think it is a song about God helping people who believe in him. Others think it is a song about having the **courage** to stand up for what they believe. No matter what people think, it is a song that talks about truth and not giving up. It is a song that will continue to be remembered and enjoyed.

What Does It Mean?

“Battle Hymn of the Republic” is a song with many meanings today. Its original meaning is most important, though. Julia Ward Howe wrote the song’s words to encourage soldiers. These men were fighting a difficult war. The words and **melody** gave soldiers strength. The marching song helped them continue fighting in tough times. It also helped them remember what they were fighting for. However, the song has some very old-fashioned words. Can you understand the song better by knowing what some of these words mean?

Words to Know

burnished Shiny.
contemners People who don’t like other people.
jubilant Happy.
loosed Unleashed.
trampling Stomping over.
writ Written.

Before the Civil War, many Southern farmers had slaves who worked the fields. Slavery was wrong. This illustration shows slaves picking cotton.

CHAPTER 2

The History of "The Battle Hymn of the Republic"

The words to "Battle Hymn" were written at the beginning of the Civil War. The Civil War was an important war in the United States. It happened from 1861 to 1865. Soldiers from

Northern states fought soldiers from Southern states. One of the reasons why they fought was to end slavery. Slavery had been in the United States since the 1600s. Many men, women, and children were slaves in the 1800s. By then, most slaves lived in the Southern part of the United States.

In 1861, a woman named Julia Ward Howe visited a Northern army camp in Washington, DC. An army camp was where soldiers lived during the war. Howe and her husband were invited to the camp by President Abraham Lincoln because they were **abolitionists**. They wanted slaves to be free. Howe was also a writer.

While she was there, Howe was inspired by the soldiers she met. She saw that they had courage. On the way back to their hotel, Howe and the other people she was traveling with sang songs. One song

This is a photograph of Julia Ward Howe. She worked hard during the Civil War to help others.

was "John Brown's Body." A **minister** also on the trip thought Howe should write new words to the song.

An Old Song with New Words

"John Brown's Body" was a popular song early in the Civil War. It talked about a real man named John Brown. He was an abolitionist. He died in 1859 after being captured during a fight with Southern soldiers. He was fighting to free slaves. Many soldiers in the Civil War liked John Brown. They also liked singing "John Brown's Body."

This is a portrait of John Brown. Like Howe, Brown was an abolitionist. He fought for the end of slavery.

"John Brown's Body" was based on a song called "Say, Brothers, Will You Meet Us?" It was written in 1856 by William Steffe. Lots of people liked Steffe's melody. Soon, other people wrote different

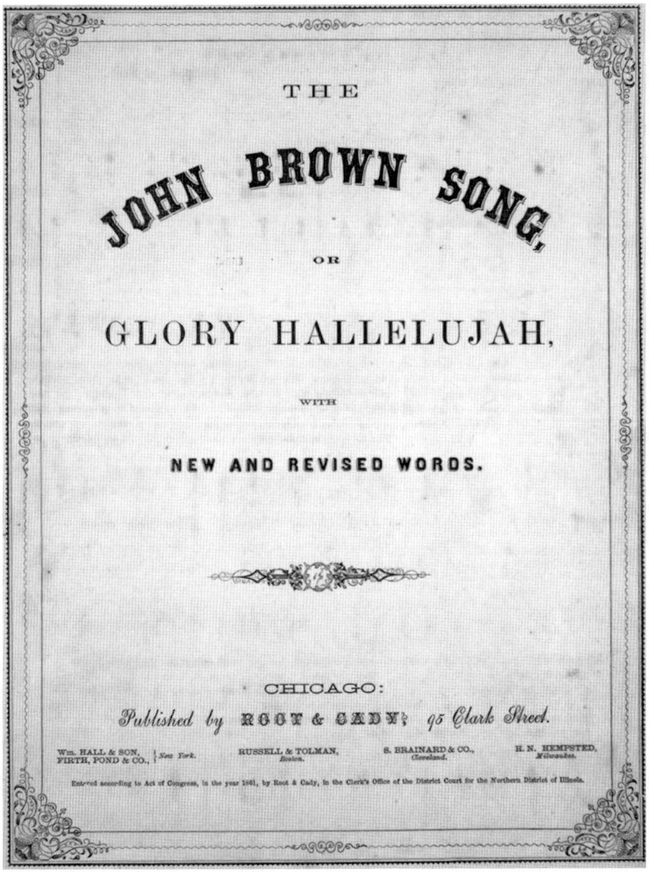

"John Brown's Body," called "The John Brown Song" here, inspired Julia Ward Howe in 1861.

words to the song. "John Brown's Body" was one popular version.

Julia Ward Howe decided to write new words too. The soldiers liked the new words she wrote. In 1862, the magazine *Atlantic Monthly* published Howe's words with the melody to "John Brown's Body." The song was on the magazine's front cover. Soon, people started singing Howe's words with Steffe's melody. They sang the song on the battlefield. They sang it in army camps. They helped the song become popular.

FACT

The only words from Steffe's original song that remain in all versions of the song are "Glory, glory, hallelujah!"

Author of "Battle Hymn"

Before she wrote "Battle Hymn," Howe was an editor writing for a newspaper called the *Commonwealth*. It

This copy of the sheet music for "Battle Hymn" was printed in 1862, soon after Howe's words first appeared on the cover of the *Atlantic Monthly*.

> **FACT**
> In 1862, the *Atlantic Monthly* paid Julia Ward Howe $5 (around $124 in 2018) for publishing "Battle Hymn."

talked about freedom for slaves. Howe enjoyed writing and talking about ending slavery. Her husband wanted to end slavery too. However, he didn't like her writing. Howe and her husband fought a lot. Still, Howe wrote articles and poems. Others liked her writing. Howe was a woman who worked hard for what she believed in.

A Patriotic Song

"Battle Hymn of the Republic" became an official song of the Northern army in the Civil War. After the war, it became a patriotic song. Many people are still inspired by the song today.

Timeline

- **1830s–1860s** The abolitionist **movement,** which tried to end slavery, becomes popular in the United States.
- **1856** William Steffe writes the song "Say, Brothers, Will You Meet Us?" It becomes known as "John Brown's Body" (with different lyrics) in 1859 and later "Battle Hymn of the Republic."
- **April 1861** The American Civil War starts after shots are fired at Fort Sumter in South Carolina.
- **November 1861** Julia Howe and her husband visit army camps near Washington, DC. Howe is inspired to write "Battle Hymn of the Republic."
- **1862** The *Atlantic Monthly* publishes Howe's lyrics on its cover.
- **1865** The Civil War ends.
- **1860s–Present** "Battle Hymn of the Republic" becomes known as a patriotic song for Americans everywhere.

"Battle Hymn" is played at different events. This military band plays the song during a Veterans Day concert.

CHAPTER 3

The Song Keeps Marching On

Today, "Battle Hymn" is still an important song in America. In fact, it is so well known that many people don't know it is William Steffe's music that they are listening to. Lots of people only know the melody as "Battle Hymn of the Republic."

The melody is played at important times of the year. You hear the words sung on the Fourth of

July. People also hear it played on **Veterans Day**. Sometimes the song is played in churches and at funerals.

Everyone's Song

"Battle Hymn" is a song for everyone. People can always find a reason to like the song. Some people

FACT

In the 1970s, women rewrote the words to "Battle Hymn" to talk about their struggle for equal rights. The song was called "The Battle Hymn of Women."

These people are standing up for women's rights and the end to the Vietnam War in 1970.

like the song because it talks about God. Others like it because the words give them strength. Many people enjoy it because it has a good message and a happy melody.

These women are singing patriotic songs together during a Memorial Day celebration in Albuquerque, New Mexico.

It is a song that has also inspired other versions of itself. Just like Julia Ward Howe did, people write new words to William Steffe's melody all the time. Sometimes they reimagine Steffe's tune. An example is jazz musician

FACT

Julia Ward Howe is remembered today. She was welcomed into the Songwriters Hall of Fame in 1970 and the National Women's Hall of Fame in 1998.

This is the entrace to the National Women's Hall of Fame in Seneca Falls, New York.

John Batiste performs in New York City in 2018.

Jon Batiste. He changed the song's melody for a podcast in 2017.

Overall, "Battle Hymn of the Republic" is a song that brings people together. It is a song that will inspire and encourage people for a long time.

Famous Uses

Joined by former president George W. Bush (*first row, fourth from left*) and others, President Obama (*first row, center left*) and his wife Michelle (*left of Obama*) sing "Battle Hymn" at a service in Dallas, Texas, in 2016.

"Battle Hymn of the Republic" has been used by famous people in the 1900s and 2000s. In 1968, **civil rights activist** Martin Luther King Jr. gave a speech called "I've Been to the Mountaintop." He used the words "Mine eyes have seen the glory of the coming of the Lord." Today, the song is performed at important events. Examples are the US Naval Academy Glee Club choir performing during a Veterans Day concert in Dallas, Texas, in 2016; singer Yolanda Adams's TV performance for a Fourth of July celebration in 2017; and the St. Martin's Choir at President George H. W. Bush's funeral in 2018.

GLOSSARY

abolitionists People who wanted slaves free in the United States and tried to help them.

civil rights activist A person who works hard to get equal treatment for all people in a country.

courage Another word for bravery.

melody The main part in a piece of music that people sing.

minister A leader of a church.

movement A time in history where lots of people are working together to reach a certain goal, like freedom or equality.

patriotic Relating to love of a country.

Veterans Day November 11, the day when soldiers who have fought in all wars around the world are remembered.

FIND OUT MORE

Books

Raum, Elizabeth. *Julia Ward Howe*. American Lives. Portsmouth, NH: Heinemann, 2004.

Women Abolitionists: Harriet Beecher Stowe, Julia Ward Howe, and Lucy Stone. New York: Oakley Press, 2011.

Websites

Britannica Kids: Julia Ward Howe

https://kids.britannica.com/students/article/Julia-Ward-Howe/311745

This website gives a brief biography about Julia Ward Howe.

Songwriters Hall of Fame: Julia Ward Howe

https://www.songhall.org/profile/Julia_Ward_Howe

Read all about Julia Ward Howe at the Songwriters Hall of Fame's official web page for her.

Videos

Cooltime Kids: The Battle Hymn of the Republic

https://www.youtube.com/watch?v=-N8Le7p0brE

Listen to kids sing the words to Julia Ward Howe's poem "Battle Hymn of the Republic."

PBS NewsHour: St. Martin's Choir Sings "Battle Hymn" at President George H. W. Bush's Funeral

https://www.youtube.com/watch?v=TULxyHRgrw4

Listen and watch as St. Martin's Choir of Houston, Texas, sings the song during President George H. W. Bush's funeral in 2018. A band also plays, giving the song extra emotion.

INDEX

Page numbers in **boldface** refer to images. Entries in **boldface** are glossary terms.

abolitionists, 14, 16, 21
Adams, Yolanda, 27
Atlantic Monthly, 18, 20–21
Batiste, Jon, 25–26, **26**
Brown, John, 16, **16**
civil rights activist, 27
Civil War, 8–9, **8**, **9**, 13–14, 16, 18, 20–21
courage, 10, 14
Fourth of July, 23–24, 27
funerals, 24, 27
Howe, Julia Ward, 8–9, 11, 14, **15**, 16, 18, 20–21, 25–26
"John Brown's Body," 16–18, **17**, 21
King, Martin Luther, Jr., 27
Lincoln, Abraham, 14
lyrics (complete), 6–7
meaning of song, 8, 10–11, 25
melody, 11, 17–18, 23, 25–26
minister, 16
movement, 21
parades, 10, **10**
patriotic, 10, 20–21
"Say, Brothers, Will You Meet Us?," 17, 21
sheet music, 6, **17**, **19**, **22**
slavery, 9, **12**, 14, 16, 20–21
Steffe, William, 17–18, 21, 23, 25
Veterans Day, **22**, 24, 27
women's rights, 24, 24

ABOUT THE AUTHOR

Kristen Susienka earned her bachelor's in English from St. Norbert College in De Pere, Wisconsin. She later received her master's in publishing. She is an avid reader, writer, and runner living in Western New York. One of her favorite things to do is sing. She also loves learning about the songs of the past.